THE PLAY
ABOUT
THE BABY

THE PLAY
ABOUT
THE BABY

Edward Albee

THE OVERLOOK PRESS
WOODSTOCK & NEW YORK

First published in paperback in the United States in 2004 by
The Overlook Press, Peter Mayer Publishers, Inc.
Woodstock & New York

WOODSTOCK:
One Overlook Drive
Woodstock, NY 12498
www.overlookpress.com
[for individual orders, bulk and special sales, contact our Woodstock office]

NEW YORK:
141 Wooster Street
New York, NY 10012

Library of Congress Cataloging-in-Publication Data

Albee, Edward, 1928-
The play about the baby / by Edward Albee.
p. cm.
1. Infants—Drama. 2. Parent and child—Drama. 3. Loss (Psychology)—Drama. I. Title.
PS3551.L25 P58 2003   812'.54—dc21   2002034639

Book design and type formatting by Bernard Schleifer
Manufactured in the United States of America
FIRST EDITION
1 3 5 7 9 8 6 4 2
ISBN 1-58567-511-3

THE PLAY
ABOUT
THE BABY

The Play About the Baby was given its world-premiere production, directed by Howard Davies, at London's Almeida Theatre in 1998.

The Play About the Baby—in a production directed by Edward Albee—was originally produced in the United States in April 2000 by the Alley Theatre, Gregory Boyd, artistic director, Paul R. Tetreault, managing director.

The Play About the Baby premiered in New York City at the Century Center for the Performing Arts on February 1, 2001, produced by Elizabeth Ireland McCann, Daryl Roth, Terry Allen Kramer, Fifty-Second Street Productions, Robert Bartner, and Stanley Kaufelt, in association with the Alley Theatre. David Esbjornson was the director, John Arnone designed the set, Michael Krass designed the costumes, and Kenneth Posner did the lighting design. The production manager was Kai Brothers, and the production stage manager Lloyd Davis, Jr. The cast was as follows:

Girl	*Kathleen Early*
Boy	*David Burtka*
Man	*Brian Murray*
Woman	*Marian Seldes*

Act One

(*Two chairs, identically placed not far from center, slightly diagonally toward one another, walking space between them. Nice light; neutral background.*)

(BOY *and* GIRL *both seated,* girl *hugely pregnant, she stage right, he stage left; hands folded, facing out*)

GIRL

(*Not moving; calm*) I'm going to have the baby now.

(BOY *and* GIRL *exit left*)

(*Sound: Growing labor; medical preps and encouragement. Growing pain and moaning; screams with accompanying sounds; slap; baby crying. Silence.*)

(BOY *and* GIRL, *no longer pregnant, enter.*)

GIRL

(*Quietly*) There.

BOY

(*No comment*) It's the miracle of life.

GIRL

Yes; yes; it is.

BOY

(*Turns to her*) Did it hurt a lot?

GIRL

(*Touches her dress at the knee*) They say you can't remember pain.

BOY

Aha.

GIRL

(*Pause*) Yes; yes, it did.

BOY

You *can*, then.

GIRL

As I remember.

BOY

I broke my arm before I knew you. Did you know that?

GIRL

Not that I remember.

BOY

Yes. Well, I did.

(*Sound: cry of baby offstage left*)

GIRL

(*Rises*) Feeding time.

BOY

In here.

GIRL

All right. (*Exits left, behind* BOY)

BOY

(*Sort of to her, but as if she were still there*) It wasn't exactly I broke it; it was more they broke it for me. Not that they said we'll break it *for* you if you *want* us to—if you can't do it for your*self*. (*Considers*) More they just broke it—not *for* me, but rather as if I'd asked, though I hadn't. They did break it, though I hadn't asked. (*Afterthought*) I'm sure if I'd asked they would have been . . . well, eager, I guess. That's only a supposition, though.

(GIRL *reenters from left, already feeding the baby; she sits again, chair right. We do not see it, merely its blanket.*)

GIRL

Very hungry.

BOY

I'll want some; remember.

GIRL

(*Slightly ironic*) Line up!

BOY

(*Matter-of-fact*) I'd come from the gym and I was pumped.

GIRL

(*Looking down*) V . . . e . . . r . . . y hungry.

BOY

The bloodrush, the endorphins . . .

GIRL

(*To* BOY) I love your body; I really do.

BOY

(*Little wiggle of eyebrows*) I know; I know you do. (*Back to previous tone*) . . . and I was walking back to the dorm, and I had my gym bag and my stuff and I was . . .

GIRL

When you let me lick your armpits I almost faint, I really do.

BOY

It tickles.

GIRL

(*Smiles*) You start getting hard.

BOY

Yes: it tickles. (*Previous tone*) And I was in the alley between the gym and the science building and there were these guys I'd seen at the Hopeless Mothers gig at the arena when I was taking tickets there? And I'd spotted them trying to sneak in and I'd called the guards on them . . .

GIRL

I like your left armpit better than the other.

BOY

Well, the other arm got broken; I was *telling* you.

GIRL

You think that's . . . Ow! (*Reaction to baby at breast*)

BOY

Let *me* at it for a while. *I* won't bite!

GIRL

(*Oddly*) Not now.

BOY

I think I like both your breasts equally.

GIRL

What happened?

BOY

Hm?

GIRL

You called the guards on them—on the guys.

BOY

Oh, and the guards roughed them up a little, and they said "We'll get you, motherfucker!" The guys—not the guards. To me; they said it to me.

GIRL

(*Looks at him*) Yes: of course the guys, and of course to you.

BOY

And that's what they did.

GIRL

What?

BOY

They got me, motherfucker. They said, in the alley there, hey, you're the one put the guard dogs on us, aren't you. I said yes, I was; guards, not guard dogs.

GIRL

Not a wise answer.

BOY

Which?

GIRL

Either; both.

BOY

Never lie. Besides, they knew. Yes, I am, I said. You guys could have paid—benefit and all. You guys could have paid.

GIRL

What was the benefit?

BOY

Mother's Milk.

GIRL

Ah.

BOY

Yeah, I know, I know, they said—kind of apologetic; we shoulda paid. No hard feelings I said. Hey, no way, no way, they said. And I put my hand out: no hard feelings I said.

GIRL

Less wise.

BOY

I know; and I think I knew what was going to happen, but too quick to stop it.

GIRL

(*Looks at baby*) Baby's full. (*Rises, goes off left, behind* BOY)

BOY

(*As she exits; as previously*) I put my hand out, and I'd just come from the gym and my forearms looked great. (*Begins to demonstrate*) And the big guy put his hand out and shook hands with me and swung around and cracked my arm against his knee and . . . Crack! And oh shit it hurt! Have fun taking tickets, the big one said, and the others laughed, and I was on my knees, and it hurt so much I was crying, and one of the others came up on me, and he unzipped his fly and what was he going to do . . . piss on me? I don't know; and the big one said leave him alone and they walked off. (*Pause*) Maybe he *wasn't* going to piss on me; maybe he was going to . . .

(GIRL *reenters from left*)

GIRL

All asleep. (*Observes him on his knees, his disturbance*)

BOY

(*Still preoccupied*) I don't know what he was going to do! It hurt so! They hurt me so!

GIRL

(*She kneels in front of him, baring a breast.*) Shhhhhhh.

BOY

(*Softly; almost pleading*) He hurt me so.

GIRL

Come toward *me*.

BOY

(*His left hand on her breast, his right arm hanging limp; still on his knees*) . . . and the other one came toward me . . .

GIRL

Here. Do this.

BOY

(*His words becoming mumble as he fastens his mouth on her breast*) . . . and he undid his fly, and I don't know what he was going to do. I don't know if he was going to . . .

GIRL

Shhhhh. Shhhhh. Shhhhh. Come. In here, in here.

(GIRL *leads* BOY *off left.* MAN *enters, comes center and stands behind and between the chairs.*)

MAN

(*Out; smile*) Hello there! (*Gestures off left.*) Boy, girl? Yes?

> (MAN *observes chairs; passes fingers of right hand over stage-right chair; smells fingers; considers; looks off left. Addresses audience; sighs.*)

Ah . . . youngsmell! Have you ever noticed when you're driving somewhere you've not been before—directions, of course —it always takes longer than you think it should, that you've passed it, or not turned left when you were supposed to? And yet, when you're coming home, or whatever, *after* you've been there—the place you didn't know how to get to, but had directions—you're amazed at how much shorter the trip is? (*Fingers of left hand over stage-left chair; smells fingers; eyebrows waggling; whispers*) Youngsmell. Have you noticed that? Not youngsmell; how much shorter the trip is? I'm not sure whether it's it *does* take longer to get there, or it's it just seems so. (*To someone in particular*) Have you noticed that? Hm? (*If no answer, go on; if there's an answer, improvise briefly.*) I don't think it's merely that it *seems* so, though it may seem that way—which may be the same thing but I don't think so: that which we *feel* we've experienced is the same as we have? (*Dismissive*) Naaaaah! Reality determined by our experience of it? Or our *sense* of experiencing it? Naaaaaaah!

(*Smells both hands together, then right, then left, then both again.*) Eeny-meeny-miney-moe! Have you ever noticed when you're talking to someone you should know, but don't, at a cocktail party, say, and you try to lead the conversation to remind you who they are—who you're talking to—they won't do it? They won't let you go there? Do they know what you're trying to do and are doing a kind of "Fuck you. You don't remember me? Well, fuck you; just hang there!" Or are they so absorbed seeing you again, remembering *you*—perfectly, of course: your name, the stuff you did to your wife—that it would never occur to them you're twisting in the wind? Once, I was at a party; well, no, I was *giving* it, and I was being a good host—introducing people to people, putting types together I thought would be good for one another or, sometimes, just a hoot, or plain wrong—and I'd been at it for a while—it was a big party—and I was groggy, I guess, and there was this tall, older woman next to me—she'd sort of come over from another group—and two dykes came up—middle-aged, neither one diesel, neither one lipstick, real centered ladies— and I'd known them for years, and they were Jo and Lu, good simple, nonspecific names: none of this Josephine and Lucille shit—and I did my host act, and I turned to introduce them to the older woman standing next to me, and I looked at her, and I knew she was familiar, but I couldn't, for the life of me, remember who she was, and I said, "Jo, Lu, this is . . . this is . . . " and Jo laughed and said, "We *know* your *mother*, dear." (*To someone specific*) Fall through the floor!! Ever done that!? (*General again*) I suppose that was the worst—so far!, though I'm looking forward with a kind of dread—fascinated dread, you know? After Jo and Lu had chuckled off, Mother looked at me sort of funny and said, "You didn't know who I was, did you?" "Oh, come on, Ma!" I said, hearty guffaw. "No, you didn't," she said, just the fringiest little bit sad, and she walked away. It didn't *change* anything between us; we were O.K., but I think it was the first time I realized we were both adults. She died three years later. (*To someone in particular; laughing*) No! Not from that! (*General again*) *Nobody* dies from not being remembered. (*Change of tone; more interior*) From being forgotten, yes, very probably, but not from not being remembered. (*Pause*) Or are they the same *thing*? (*Thinks*) No; not quite. (*Energy rising*) So! Anyway! I bring all this up

because . . . well, clearly because I wanted to bring it up, and
I dare say there was a . . . Yes! Of course! Driving somewhere
you'd never been before, that was it; that started it all. (*Smells
fingers of both hands again*) Ahhh! How things fade—memo-
ries, photo-memories sometimes, last, though, usually. *Scent.*
(*Spells it*) S...C...E...N...T. (*Sad now*) All fades, all dissolves,
and we are left with . . . invention; *re*invention. I wonder how
I'll remember (*Gestures about him*) all of *this*? But, since I'm
not *there* yet—so to speak—have not, haven't remembered it
. . . (brisk) well, first we *invent*, and then we *re*invent. As with
the past so the future—reality, as they laughingly call it? Who
was it said "Our reality—or something—is determined by our
need? The greater need rules the game?" The reality? I guess
that was *me*. All those "naaaahs" before? Remember the
"naaaahs"? Just a trick. Pay attention to this, what's true and
what isn't is a tricky business, no? What's real and what isn't?
Tricky. Do you follow? Yes? No? Good. (*Shrugs*) Whichever.
(*Begins to exit*) Woman.

(*As* MAN *exits, stage left,* WOMAN *enters stage right, rather briskly; sees*
MAN *exiting.*)

WOMAN
(*After exiting* MAN) Wait; wait! (*He exits*) Am I late? (*To audience now*) Am I late!? Am I on time!?

(BOY *enters, wearing a towel only;* WOMAN *sees him*)

WOMAN
(*To* BOY; *concerned*) Am I late?

BOY
(*Mildly puzzled*) Hello?

WOMAN
Hello. Am I late?

BOY
(*Matter-of-fact*) I wouldn't know. (*Afterthought*) Would I?

WOMAN
(*Fretful*) I don't *know*!

BOY
(*Wipes his mouth; licks his lips; smiles*) I've been mountain climbing.

WOMAN
(*Overly bright*) Have you!

BOY
Yes.

WOMAN
You hardly seem dressed for it.

BOY
(*Looks at his towel*) Oh, I put this *on* . . . put it around me.

WOMAN
(*Tiny pause as* BOY *doesn't continue*) Oh? Aha! (*Pause*) Where? Where did you put it on? I don't mean around your waist; I mean . . . where?

BOY
(*Points left, over his shoulder*) In *there*.

WOMAN
No, I mean . . . (*Pause*) Aha. (*Pause*) Do you know who I am?

BOY
No.

WOMAN
Aha. (*Pause*) Are you certain?

BOY
I'm not?

WOMAN
Aha. (*Silence*) *Mountain* climbing?

BOY

(*Recalling; eyes closed, perhaps?*) It's all jungle as you approach—well, as you imagine it: warm, warmer, moist; but you move through it, past all that, eventually, reluctantly, of course; you're coming up from the south—from below—and you see them up ahead, looming, but there is a lot to get through first, as I said, in the jungle there—the ridges, and the great declivity. God!, and it's so hot and moist and . . . and . . . thrilling, and . . .

WOMAN

I've never done it.

BOY

(*Looks at her oddly*) Oh? (*Considers it*) Well, quite probably not; not too many women do . . . what? Ten percent? I mean: I don't know you. (*Afterthought*) Do I? (*Answers his own question*) No; no, I don't think I do. So, no, you may not have—certainly not these; certainly not. (*Holds invisible melons toward her; on with his story*) And . . . do you mind if I get hyperbolic here? Even *more* hyperbolic?

WOMAN

(*Cautious*) I don't . . . *think* so.

BOY

Even more than I have been? I didn't think you would. And there are the deep ravines, and the ridges, and there are a lot of temptations! Well, one in particular—two! Two!! And you *do* stop there on your climb, on your ascent.

WOMAN

To rest.

BOY

Oh? (*Chuckles*) No, not exactly; more to delve, I guess; to explore; to absorb; to die a little. But you look up—over the great sloping hill with all its jungle, and there they are! (*Sighs*) My goodness, there they are.

WOMAN

(*Helping*) Snow-capped, jagged . . .

BOY
(*Slightly more disapproving*) Who *are* you, lady!?

WOMAN
Not snowcapped? *Not* jagged?

BOY
(*Quiet*) No; of course not: lovely, curving slopes, almost twins. You go between them; there's moisture there; you breathe; you press your ears gently between them and it's the sound of giant seashells.

WOMAN
(*Gets it*) Ohhhhhh! Ohhhhh, I see! *Those* mountains; *that* climbing.

BOY
(*Puzzled*) Yes, of course. What else?

WOMAN
(*Half to the* BOY, *half to herself*) Hyperbole: of course. (*Out*) I should have known.
(GIRL *appears from left, naked, or as naked as the actress will allow*)

GIRL
(*To* BOY) What are you doing? Are you coming back in? What are you doing?

BOY
(*Over his shoulder*) Yes; right away.

GIRL
(*Pointing to* WOMAN) Who is that?

BOY
(*Simply*) I don't know.

GIRL
(*Considers it*) Oh. (*Considers it further*) Well, leave her there where you found her and come back in. You're not finished; you're not there yet.

BOY

(*Backing left*) Yes, I know. (*To* WOMAN *now*) Yes; goodbye; I'm
not there yet.

(*They exit*—BOY *and* GIRL—*leaving* WOMAN *standing.*)

WOMAN

(*Waves*) Farewell, intrepid traveler. (*Waves off*) Farewell!
(*Out*) Where there's a boy, there's a girl, no? (*Shrugs*) Usually.
(*Looks at the audience*) Well. I . . . uh . . . well, I suppose
you'd like to know who I am, or why I'm here. (*Some uncer-
tainty*) Well, I'm with *him* (*gestures off left*); that's why I'm
here; I'm with him. The man; not the boy. The man indicated
me as he exited, said "Woman" and exited. Remember? That's
why I'm here—to be with him. To help . . . *him*; to . . . assist
him. (*Hand up, palm out, to abort protest*) I'm not an actress;
I want you to know that right off, though why you'd think I
was, I mean automatically think I *was*, I don't know, though I
am a trifle . . . theatrical, I suppose, and no apologies *there*. I
was Prince Charming in our all-girl school production of Snow
White, and while the bug may have bitten, it never took.
(*Chuckles*) Nor—and forgive the seeming discontinuity
here—nor am I from the press. That's the first thing I want
you to know—well, the second, actually, the first being . . .
having been . . . (*Trails off; starts again*) Oh, I am a very good
cook, among other things. I became that to please my husband, my *then* husband, who was in the habit of eating out, by
which he meant . . . alone . . . without *me*. It occurred to *me* that
if I . . . well, it was no good: alone, to him, meant *specifically* not
with *me*, though with others, with lots of others. And the great
feasts I'd prepare . . . would be for *me*. Alone. I became quite
heavy, which I no longer am, and unmarried, which I am to
this day. I trust he is still eating alone . . . all by himself . . .
facing a wall. (*Pause*) No matter. Really: from the very first
week, come dinnertime, he would put the paper under his
arm, say "Bye, bye," or whatever, and . . . no matter. I *have*
had journalistic dreams, though I am not a journalist—dreams
of *being* a journalist, that is, and quite awake; not asleep. I
went so far one time as to take a course; and my assignment
was to interview a *writer*, to try to comprehend the "creative
mind" as they call it. (*Firm gesture*) Don't try! Don't even give
it a thought! There seems to be some sort of cabal going on

on the part of these so-called creative people to keep the process a secret—a deep dark secret—from the rest of the world. What's the matter with these people? Do they think we're trying to steal their tricks? . . . would even *want* to!? And all I wanted to do was . . . under*stand*! And, let me tell you!, getting through to them—the creative types?—isn't easy. I mean even getting *at* them. I wrote politely to seven or eight of them, two poets, one biographer, a couple of short story writers, one female creator of "theatre pieces," et cetera, and not one of them answered. Silence; too busy "creating," I guess. (*On a roll now*) I remember finally I bribed someone into giving me this one guy's agent's name—this novelist?— and persuaded the agent to call him and see if *I* could *call* him?, and maybe *talk* to him?, and finding out I could *do* that—with no guarantees, naturally—and calling, and hitting the brick wall of the novelist's male secretary. I don't *mean* anything by that, of course. (*Heavy wink*) In any event, hitting *that* brick wall, having to repeat everything I'd said to the agent, and being told by the M.S.—the male secretary (*Heavy wink*)—they'd get back to me, and waiting until finally they *did*—I mean, *really*, who did they think they were . . . *both* of them!? Finally, the M.S. *did* call me—I was in the touchy stages of a soufflé, naturally—telling me that *he* was there . . . (*does fingers as quotes*) "Himself" that is: the famous novelist . . . and he *was* going to talk to me —"himself" was—and I held the receiver to my ear, expecting what?—something other than a voice? I don't know—a choir of some sort? I held, and then his voice came . . . "here I am," it said—*he* said— "here I am." Odd, no? And the voice wasn't friendly, or un- friendly, gruffer than I'd thought it would be, perhaps, just . . . noncommittal. "Here I am; I'm here." I almost hung up, but I didn't. I mean, I'd gotten this close, and if I hung up who *knows* when I'd get another . . . *you* know. "I'm here," he said. And I rushed through what I wanted. "I'm studying the cre- ative process, and I want to do it with *you*, through *you*— watching *you*, understanding *you*." "You want to watch me while I *write*?!" he said, sort of incredulous, and I could sense the phone being passed back to the M.S., or just hung up, or tossed over his shoulder, or whatever. "No! Wait!" I yelled. Silence. "I'm waiting," he finally said, no emotion at all. And I tried to explain what I really wanted.

(GIRL, *chased by* BOY—*naked, or close—goes from
stage left to stage right, a sweet chase, giggling, etc.*
WOMAN *senses, sees them.*)

What?! What was that?! Did two people just run nakedly
across the stage, giggling? Yes? Well . . . why not? Where was
I? Oh: "What I really want is to watch you . . . uh . . . move
your words from your mind to the page." "You're not serious,"
he said, sort of . . . fading away. "Oh, wait! Please; please!" I
said—shouted, really. "I *do* want to study you! I so want to
watch you move your words from your mind to the page." The
sentence was beginning to sound strange to me. I heard a kind
of chuckle from him . . . bitter, was it? Contemptuous? "Well,
that wouldn't be much fun for anybody but *you, would* it . . .
you underfoot, banging into people, asking a lot of ridiculous
questions, studying everything, being an absolute . . ." "I'd be
a mouse! I'd be a mouse!" I said—(*Shrugs*) mouse-like, I suppose. "Yeah, sure!" he guffawed at me, right over the phone.
"Oh please; oh, please!" I whimpered. (*An aside*) Have you
ever noticed the way we say everything twice when we're
upset? "I'll be a mouse, I'll be a mouse." "Oh, please, oh,
please!" Have you noticed that? *I* have. "Will you? Will you?
It'll only take a couple of weeks, and . . . " "I'd rather die," he
said quietly . . . and he hung up. (*Indignation*) What kind of
people *are* they?! I mean . . . what kind of people *are* they,
these . . . these . . .

(GIRL *and* BOY *repeat their previous stage cross,
but from stage right to stage left.*)

(*Noticing*) Two people just ran nakedly across the stage again,
did they not? Giggling? No? (*Businesslike*) Well, then; now
you know who I am *not*, what I do *not* do. As for who I am
and what I *do* do, stay tuned.

(MAN *enters*)

You've had me standing out here, vamping away . . .

MAN

(*Amused*) Shhhhhhhh; shhhhhhhh. It's fine; it's fine. Come
along now.

WOMAN

What were you doing?

MAN

Research? Peeing? Reparking? Whatever. (*Indicates off left*)
Boy and girl.

WOMAN

Yes; I noticed.

MAN

That's them. "That's they" doesn't sound right, though it is.

WOMAN

No, it doesn't. That is them, eh?

MAN

Yes. How innocent they are.

WOMAN

Yes.

MAN

Pure.

WOMAN

Yes.

MAN

You'd think it was Eden, wouldn't you.

WOMAN

Yes. You would.

MAN

Yes. (*Takes her hand; indicates out*) Say bye-bye.

WOMAN

(*Out*) Bye-bye.
(*They exit.* GIRL, *followed by* BOY, *comes out, peers after* WOMAN.)

GIRL

Who *is* she? Who *is* that woman?

BOY

(*Looking after her*) Very strange.

GIRL

Yes.

BOY

I tried to talk to her. (*Correcting himself*) *She* tried to talk to
me.

GIRL

And?

BOY

Very strange. She asked me if I knew who she was.

GIRL

What did you tell her?

BOY

That I didn't.

GIRL

Maybe she'll go away.

BOY

Maybe. (*Smiles*) Can I chase you some more?

GIRL

(*Giggles*) No! No, you can't! It was fun!

BOY

Yes; yes it was. (*Decision*) I'm going to chase you some more.

GIRL

(*Delighted*) You'll catch me. I'll let you catch me.

BOY

Will you let me roll you over, lay you down, and do it again?

GIRL

(*Giggles*) Maybe. (*Shyly sings:*) Roll me over,
In the clover
Roll me over
Lay me down

BOY

(*Joins in; they both sing.*)   And do it again.

BOY

I like being on you.

GIRL

(*Nice*) I've noticed.

BOY

I like being *in* you. (*Quickly*) You've noticed; yes, I know.

GIRL

Yes.

BOY

I like sleeping with you.

GIRL

Yes.

BOY

(*A smile*) I like sleeping *in* you.

GIRL

Yes.

BOY

Saves time.

GIRL

Yes. Who *is* she? Who *is* that woman?

BOY

Is she familiar?

GIRL

No, not exactly. I mean, she looks like a *woman*, but no; not at all; not familiar at all. (*An afterthought*) A photograph, maybe?

BOY

(*Shrugs*) She looks like a lot of people.

GIRL

Yes. (*Abruptly*) *Does* she?

BOY

You don't. *You* look like *you*.

GIRL

(*Preoccupied*) Oh? Does that make me happy?

BOY

It should.

GIRL

Oh, well, then, it probably does.

BOY

(*Takes her wrist*) Come with me.

GIRL

(*Mild concern*) Where?

BOY

In there. (*Indicates stage left*) I want to *do* something.

GIRL

(*Greater concern*) What?!

BOY

Something new; something we've never done.

GIRL

(*Slightly worried*) There *isn't* anything.

BOY

(*Pulling her*) I *read* about something. Don't fight me.

GIRL

(*Some alarm*) What *is* it?! What is it you want to do?

BOY

Relax into it. (*Lets her wrist go; hands to his chest, mock eloquence*) You're my goal; you're my destination. You are my moon and sun and earth and sky and . . . (*breaks tone*) on and on, and so on and so forth. (*Grabs her wrist again*) C'mon!

GIRL

No! What! What *is* it?!

BOY

(*An enthusiastic confidence*) It hasn't been done for centuries; three religions outlawed it in the Middle Ages. C'mon!

GIRL

(*Reluctantly giving in*) W . . . e . . . l . . . l.

BOY

You'll *love* it. (*Mock tone again*) You are my goal; you are my destination. (*Normal tone again*) C'mon, girl, let's go!

GIRL

(*Allowing herself to be dragged off*) Not in front of the baby; whatever it is, not in front of the baby.

BOY

(*Slightly annoyed, as they exit*) Okay; okay.

(*After* BOY *and* GIRL *exit,* MAN *enters from right, playing blind.*)

MAN

(*To the audience, but not looking at it, of course, and not facing it.*) The chairs should be right ahead of me . . . right . . . *here!* (*Wrong*) No. Further? (*Bumps against stage-right chair*) Ow! Yes; there it is. (*Opens eyes, turns to face audience*) Did she give you a good time? Spin a splendid yarn? Yes? Good. She's good at that; she's very good at that. Have you ever done this?—pretended to be blind? I don't mean to offend those of you in the audience who *are* blind—physically blind, that is—though there are seldom many of you at plays—*blind*; deaf, yes; blind, seldom; which surprises me, since most good plays come at you "by the ear," so to speak; but, then again, so do a lot of bad ones—by the ear. The tactile is underdeveloped in the sighted—in the seeing—for the most part. I was at a museum in London a few years ago—at the Royal Academy, I *think*—and I came upon a sculpture exhibit set up especially for the blind. There were maybe twenty pieces in the exhibit—faces, abstract forms, a few animals—and there were guides about to help the blind get *to* the pieces; there were roped walkways, as well. The blind were asked to touch the sculptures, investigate them, while the guides would assist—the name of the artist, the materials, the subject if need be. I watched for a little, saw the wonder, the enthusiasm of the blind, their smiles, little cries, and then I decided to do it myself—be blind and go through the exhibit by touch only. I closed my eyes, and a guide came up to me, to help me. "I'm not blind," I said, "except I'm pretending to be, to see it, so to speak, as a blind person would. Will you help me?" This being Britain—*or* me being lucky—she chirped at me: "Of course! But be sure you keep your eyes tight shut!" And so I did, and it was fascinating—to see with my fingers, with my hands, to touch, as we sighted do in the dark, the way the blind do in their endless dark—in *their* light. There was a copy of that famous bronze sculpture of the wild boar in Florence, the one sitting on its haunches, front legs up? (*Demonstrates with his arms*) The one with the bronze penis rubbed golden by the hundreds of years of Florentine men touching it—for good luck, for potency. (*Wonders*) What about the women? Do *they* touch it? Have they touched it for centuries, at night, perhaps, in the dark? "You're coming upon the Florentine boar," she chirped—really, she *chirped*. "Be sure you touch its bits and pieces, for good luck." "Its *what*?" I said. "Its . . . you know, its *thing*," she said. "Oh, right," I said. I'd done it in Florence when I was there; but this was different; this felt very different. (*Sudden shift; very offhand*) Have you seen the baby? Cute, no? They love it, *don't* they—the baby. (*Some puzzlement*) They really *love* it. I wonder how much they love it? How much they need it? Perhaps we should find out. As the lady said, stay tuned. (*Puzzles more*) Hunh! (*A beat*) Ah, well; off we go.

(MAN *exits.* GIRL *enters, speaks off to* BOY.)

GIRL

That wasn't funny! Well, certainly not as funny as you thought it was—was going to be.

BOY

(*Entering*) Sorry. (*Not really*)

GIRL

It wasn't!

BOY

Sorry!

GIRL

Mean it!

BOY

(*Genuine*) Sorry.

GIRL

(*Grudging*) Well . . . maybe. I don't think I *like* being thought of as a destination, by the way.

BOY

(*Nice*) What would you *like* me to think of you as—if not as a destination? I always *aim* for you: you *are* a destination—*my* destination. I remember when I saw you for the first time—when I was biking along—I saw you lying there on the stretcher, all unconscious—I said—well, to myself, more than to anyone—"*That's* the one; *that's* my destination."

GIRL

(*She's heard this before.*) That's sweet.

BOY

. . . and I said to myself, "When she wakes up—if she wakes up—I'm going to be there, and I'll be the first person she sees, and she'll love me; she'll want me and she'll love me; she's my destination."

GIRL

Yes; sweet. (*More interested*) Did you *really* tell them at the hospital you were my brother? You told them you were my brother and that's why they let you in? Let you sit by me?

BOY

Yes. I wanted you very much and being your brother made it even more intense—made me hard.

GIRL

(*Not too nice*) So many things do.

BOY

(*Smiles*) Yes. Isn't that nice?

GIRL

(*Preoccupied*) I wonder how that old Gypsy knew so much?

BOY

Who, the one you went to before we met?

GIRL

Yes, the one who told me . . .

BOY

(*Sort of reciting*) What, that you would pass out one day, be put on a stretcher and taken to the hospital, where nothing was found to be wrong—if fainting away is nothing—and that when this happened you would wake up and the nurse would be over you and she would smile and say everything was just fine and that your brother was in the hospital room with you, right by your side . . . that he was hard.

GIRL

She didn't say that—either one, the nurse *or* the Gypsy—the hard part.

BOY

 . . . and that when you looked and saw it wasn't your brother . . .

GIRL

. . . not hard to determine, since I don't *have* one . . .

BOY

. . . it wasn't your brother, it would be the boy you would marry?

GIRL

Yes. I wonder how that old Gypsy knew so much?

BOY

Was she really very old? *He* very old? Gypsies look older than they are.

GIRL

(*Dogmatic*) She was *old*. That's what the sign said: "Come in and visit the old Gypsy; have your future told."

BOY

They lie.

GIRL

(*Slightly offended*) No! It was all true! It all came true!

BOY

No: about being old. It might have been a man for all *you* know.

GIRL

I can tell a man from a woman!

BOY

A Gypsy?

GIRL

(*Uncertain*) Well . . . (*More aggressive*) What do you mean "*if* she wakes up"? What do you *mean* by that?

BOY

You could have had a stroke for all *I* knew; you could have been *dead*. But you were so beautiful—so thrilling—I assumed you weren't—wouldn't be. I got off my bike—didn't even look at it, left my clips on—and saw you there and my heart sang, as the song sings. She won't be dead, I said to myself; she'll wake up and I'll be hard and she'll love me and she'll marry me.

GIRL

(*Preoccupied again*) Gypsies are strange people. How *do* they know so much?

BOY

It's easy to foretell the future: you just have to know what's going to happen.

GIRL

Hmmmmm.

BOY

And in the way of a true fairy tale come true no one even stole my bike.

GIRL

I guess those boys weren't around.

BOY

What boys?

GIRL

Oh, never mind.

BOY

Oh; those boys.

GIRL

Never *mind*. What a lovely story.

BOY

I think so. Did the Gypsy say we'd have a baby?

GIRL

No; the Gypsy was . . . well, she wouldn't *talk* about that.

BOY

Did you ask?

GIRL

Of course! "What about a baby?" I said. "What about babies? How many will we have?"

BOY

And she wouldn't say—*he* wouldn't say?

GIRL

No; she . . . the Gypsy frowned.

BOY

She *frowned*? He *frowned*?

GIRL

"I can't see that," she said; "besides: your time is up."

BOY

Your money, she meant—*he* meant: not your time, your money.

GIRL

Same thing.

BOY

Yes. With Gypsies, yes.

GIRL

Maybe we'd better go back, get some more answers; take the baby *with* us . . .

BOY

No! Gypsies steal babies!

GIRL

(*Laughing*) They don't!

BOY

You've never heard? It's famous; it's like the money scam.

GIRL

What is *that*?

BOY

You don't know? The money scam? The Gypsy promises to
double your money for you, so you bring it *to* her, or him, to
be blessed, so it'll double, or whatever. You bring it in ten dol-
lar bills, or something, in a big paper bag, and . . .

GIRL

Why do you do *that*?

BOY

What?

GIRL

Bring it to the Gypsy in a big paper bag!

BOY

To be blessed!

GIRL

No! Why in a big paper bag?

BOY

(*Mildly irritated*) Because that's the way the Gypsy *asks* for it.

GIRL

Oh.

BOY

And the Gypsy puts the paper bag . . .

GIRL

. . . with all the money in it . . .

BOY

. . . yes . . . *on* the table, between the two of you, and the
Gypsy blesses it, and starts chanting, or something, and the
music starts, and the lights go all funny . . .

GIRL

(*Losing track*) Wait a minute . . .

BOY

. . . and in the middle of all that the Gypsy pulls the famous switch.

GIRL

What famous switch?!

BOY

Hm? Oh, the famous switch of the bag. In all the chanting and the lights and the music and all, the Gypsy switches bags— takes *your* paper bag with all the money in it and puts another paper bag in its place filled with—what, I don't know—newspapers, or something, cut-up newspapers.

GIRL

(*Logical*) Well, what if you opened it?! You'd see that . . .

BOY

. . . the Gypsy tells you to bury the paper bag in your backyard without opening it and without anyone seeing you, and you're to leave it there for—what?—three weeks, so the magic can work, the money can double, or whatever.

GIRL

Yes, but . . .

BOY

. . . and you do it, because you're an asshole—you wouldn't have put your life savings in a paper bag and handed it to some damn Gypsy if you *weren't* an asshole in the first place. And so, after three weeks you go out and start digging up your backyard, since you've probably forgotten exactly where you've buried the paper bag, you being such an asshole, and your husband asks you what you're doing, and there's nothing for it, and so you say you're digging up the paper bag with all your life savings in it, like the Gypsy told you to do. And your *husband*, who knows a lot more about Gypsies than *you* do, is sitting down by now, his head in his hands, crying. And so you eventually find where you buried it, and you dig it up and you take it over to your husband to show him how the money's doubled, and you open up the bag . . .

GIRL

. . . and it's all cut-up newspaper.

BOY

Right; and the Gypsy's probably in Miami Beach by now driving around in some snazzy convertible.

GIRL

(*At a loss for words*) That's . . . that's . . . *terrible.*

BOY

You bet your life *savings* it is. So: you don't take the baby to the Gypsies.

GIRL

They'd steal it.

BOY

Probably.

GIRL

But, what would they . . . *do* with it?

BOY

(*Shrugs*) Sell it. Eat it.

GIRL

(*Disbelieving*) Noooooooo!

BOY

(*Shrugs again*) Okay.

MAN

(*Pops in*) If you're not careful you're going to have the society for the prevention of cruelty to Gypsies after you. (*Exits abruptly*)

BOY

(*To where he was; nonplussed*) Why? Why would I?

GIRL

Who *is* that *man*! Why are there so many strange people around here?

BOY

(*At* GIRL; *preoccupied*) What? What? (*To where* MAN *was*) Nobody cares about *Gypsies*! (To Girl) *What* strange people?

GIRL

You were talking to a woman earlier, and now this man sticks his head in here and . . .

BOY

(*Shrugs*) I don't know these people. I thought we were talking about the baby.

GIRL

We were; indeed we were. Do we have in-laws we don't know about?

BOY

Not that I know of.

GIRL

Have we rented out rooms?

BOY

I don't believe so.

GIRL

Then why are they here? (*Suddenly*) Maybe they're Gypsies! Come to steal the baby!

BOY

Don't *you* be silly. Do they *look* like Gypsies?

GIRL

Well . . .

BOY

Swarthy; big mustaches, cigars, fedoras . . .

GIRL

Like Mexicans?

BOY

No; different. Mexicans wear little derbies.

GIRL

That's Peruvians, and that's women.

BOY

(*Mildly annoyed*) Whatever. Mexicans look . . . Mexican. Gypsies—from photographs I've seen . . . drawings—look like . . .
well, like Gypsies.

GIRL

Oh. (*Relieved*) Then they're not Gypsies come to steal the
baby.

BOY

What I said was, these people don't *look* like Gypsies—from
what I know of how Gypsies look—which may not be much.
That's what I said. (*Pause*) Why would anybody want to steal
the baby?

GIRL

For money?

BOY

We don't have any.

GIRL

To sell it, or to eat it?

BOY

(*Sighing*) I said that's what Gypsies are *purported* to do, and I
said I didn't think that . . .

GIRL

(*Abrupt*) All *right*! (*Shy*) To *hurt* us? To injure us beyond salvation?

BOY

(*Pause; very sincere*) Aren't we too young?

GIRL

(*Not wholly convinced*) I suppose.
(*Baby crying offstage.*)

GIRL

(*Alarmed*) The baby's crying! Do you think someone is . . .

BOY

(*Comforting*) Doesn't that sound like hunger? Isn't that the hungry sound the baby makes?

GIRL

(*Somewhat relieved*) Yes; yes; I suppose so. (*Moves to exit*) I'll go feed the baby. (*Exits*)

BOY

(*Half to himself; very preoccupied*) Leave some for me. (*Pause*) (*This next speech is to "theoretical people." The audience is not to be addressed directly, nor is anyone else.*)

BOY

Beyond salvation? Injure us beyond salvation? Hurt us to the point that . . . ? (*To* GIRL, *off*) I'm standing guard. (*She doesn't hear, of course. More to himself now*) I'll guard you; I'll guard the baby. (*Gentle*) If there's anybody out there wants to do this to us—to hurt us so—ask *why*? Ask what we've *done*? I can take pain and loss and all the rest *later*—I *think* I can, when it comes as natural as . . . sleep? But . . . now? We're *happy*; we love each other; I'm hard all the time; we have a baby. We don't even under*stand* each other yet! (*Pause*) So . . . give it some thought. Give us some time. (*Pause*) O.K.?

GIRL

(*Emerges; goes to* BOY) Wasn't hungry; false alarm.

BOY

(*Shrugs*) No problem. (*Out again*) O.K.? Please?

(MAN *is propelled on stage, followed by* WOMAN; *clearly they are in the middle of a heated exchange.*)

WOMAN

I was young once, remember? I had a life before you?

MAN

Oh, God!

WOMAN

What you referred to—what you always refer to—as my privileged little life before I met you?

MAN

Oh, God! (*Indicates out*) Not in front of all these people! (*Indicates* BOY *and* GIRL *who are peripheral*) Not in front of the children!

(*They stand, sit, move; musical chairs, etc.*)

WOMAN

Well, I *did* have. You think no one but you wanted me? Hunh?! (*A pronouncement*) A painter hanged himself for the love of me.

MAN

(*Flat contradiction*) No.

WOMAN

Yes, he *did*. I was eighteen, and moving into ripeness. I was eighteen, as I said, and knowledgeable, and I was at a tea one afternoon—it was summer; it was a resort—and I had on silk and a great hat with ribbons, and I had been to Europe . . .

MAN

(*Quietly dogmatic*) You had *not*. (*To* BOY *and* GIRL) She had not!

WOMAN

(*Overriding him*) . . . and I had been to Europe, and I knew the women there went without bras if their breasts were exemplary and if they were young, and I had my lovely breasts. (*Cups them for him*) Lovely? Breasts? (*Tiny pause*) Nothing?

MAN

Get on with it.

WOMAN

(*Smiles*) And I had my lovely breasts free in the delicious silk, an unlined silk, smooth against my nipples; and I stalked about—I think I had a parasol as well, really doing it up. Very Gainsborough, or perhaps Watteau.

MAN

Jesus!

WOMAN

"Very Gainsborough, or perhaps Watteau," I heard a voice say, just behind me and to the right. I stopped. I mean, who else could the voice be referring to, right?

MAN

(*Ironic*) Right!

WOMAN

"Definitely Watteau," it went on, "definitely Watteau." And I turned my pretty head, and there he was . . . The Painter. Not a man who painted, not a painter, but . . . The Painter: hollow-cheeked, burning eyes, wispy whiskers, long, bony fingers, the voice cavernous, basso, the costume . . . well, do you know Whistler? (*Afterthought*) Of course you do.

MAN

Of course I do.

WOMAN

Of course you do.

MAN

What do you take me for?

WOMAN

"You should have a crook and sheep, or an arm basket filled with wildflowers. I'm going to paint you," he said. "*Are* you!" I said . . .

MAN

(*Out*) I don't believe a word of this. (*To* BOY *and* GIRL) Not a word of this is true.

WOMAN

"Yes," he said, "twice." "To get it right?" I joked. "First time a practice swing?" "No," he said, his burning eyes even deeper and sadder, "first as you are, as you are right now, and then, later, naked, your lovely breasts, the dimple of your belly, your milk-pink hips, your burning bush . . . " "Really!" I said. "You go too far!" Phrases like that just . . . came to me then; I could do them with conviction. "Really, Sir, you go too far."

MAN

(*Back in*) Milk-pink?

WOMAN

(*A trifle embarrassed*) Well . . . yes.

MAN

You must have read it somewhere. (*To* BOY *and* GIRL) She read it somewhere.

WOMAN

(*High horse*) It is what he said! (*Back to recounting; out*) I should probably interject here that all my lovers to that moment had been both young and handsome—sturdy, virile boys and young men my own age, well-muscled . . . handsome, as I said. I had not made love with the aged, with cripples, dwarves, or— and I blush at this, I think, in retrospect, at least, for its lack of humor, its lack of generosity—even with the simply plain.

MAN

(*Eyes to heaven*) Christ!

WOMAN

(*Back in*) Needless to say—needles, as I used to say when I was little—*almost* needles to say, nothing was further from my lovely mind than an affair with the gaunt and disheveled painter. (*Thinks*) Well . . . perhaps death was further from my mind, but not much. I was seeing—as they say—"seeing" a young polo player . . .

MAN
(*Out*) Do you believe *any* of this? (*To* BOY *and* GIRL) Do you?
(*Afterthought*) Well, *they* might.

WOMAN
Yes, of course they do . . . a young polo player, whose biceps
alone were worth the trip. I was seeing him, and quite in-
volved, almost . . . happy. What did I need with . . . well, with
anything else? My days were filled with polo, my nights with
rut. Oh, what a wangled teb we weave.

MAN
A what?

WOMAN
A teb; a wangled teb.

MAN
What is *that*?

WOMAN
You figure it out. Anyway, I sat for the painter. He was metic-
ulous, and he worked so slowly. My polo player wondered
where I was instead of watching him knock balls through the
legs of horses. "I'm being painted as a shepherdess," I said.
"You're kidding!" he replied, white teeth flashing, et cetera.
"Be careful he doesn't want to paint you in the nude," he
warned. "Oh, he does," I smiled, "he does." And Beauty's face
darkened—even beneath the tan—and my young heart broke,
for I saw that he loved me, and I knew in that moment . . .
that I did not love him.

MAN
Oh, you poor dear!

WOMAN
That I *desired* him, yes; I mean, he *was* a splendid lover—
slow, patient, thoughtful, but always in command, and driving.
Indeed, he was splendid.

MAN

(*Out*) Look at her! You believe this?

WOMAN

Of course they do. *But* . . . I became lovers with the painter.
He wasn't much good—in bed, I mean. "I know I'm unworthy
of you," he said, "That my touch is unworthy of you, that when
I crawl on you like a spider in the night, my bony fingers trem-
bling on your perfect breasts . . . "

MAN

(*To* WOMAN) Nobody talks like that!

WOMAN

He did . . . "and when you let me enter in, it is in an act of
mercy . . . "

MAN

(*Out*) Nobody! Nobody has *ever* talked like that! (*To* BOY *and*
GIRL) Nobody. EVER. Don't just stand there with your
mouths open! Learn something!

WOMAN

"I know all this and I am strengthened by my weakness." And
so on and so forth. And, well, he *was* strengthened; his talent
surged; his drawings of me—*and* the paintings—made him,
well . . . quite famous. I hang in museums. You didn't know
that, *did* you?

MAN

(*In*) You do not. (*Out*) She does not. (*To* BOY *and* GIRL) She
does not.

WOMAN

I do not? But I began to see something: that *he* was getting
far more out of this than *I* was: he had his lovely decoration,
plus a model for free, plus a source of income, and *I* was sad-
dled with this . . . skimpy little man with only bones and drive
and the oddest breath and . . . and I felt *tricked*. I be*longed*
with the polo players and such, the healthy animals.

MAN

(*Back in. Sarcastic*) Of course you did!

WOMAN

I was young and fabulous.

MAN

(*Ibid*) Yes! Of course you were!

WOMAN

And I suddenly knew that I hadn't gained the days, but I'd merely lost the nights. Do you understand? (*Waits; he merely shakes his head.*) Where was I?

MAN

Not gained the days but merely lost the nights, or some such rubbish.

WOMAN

. . . not gained the days but merely lost the nights. And so I broke it off. "You're using me," I shrieked at him, pacing his studio, knocking things over. "You don't love *me*; you love the *fact* of me." (*Shakes her head*) Who did I think I was? Who did we *all* think we were? "I can't live without you," he called to me from his window as I flounced from the building. "I'll kill myself!" "Hanh!" I said, and turned on my heel and . . . vanished into the mist, or whatever. And of course he *did*: kill himself, that is. He hanged himself in his atelier, from a rafter. (*Pause*) And how does all *that* strike you? How and where does all *that* grab you?

MAN

(*Shakes his head; smiles, applauds*) Very good! Really, very good! (*Out*) Wasn't that good? Didn't she do that well? Come on, give her a hand! (*Encourages, leads audience applause. She curtsies. If there is none, he dismisses audience with a wave of his hand.*) Good. Really very good. (*To* BOY *and* GIRL) Didn't you think so? (*Before they can reply: a sudden shift to very businesslike; in*) O.K. Let's get on with it. (*To* BOY *and* GIRL; *calling*) Will you two come over here, please?

BOY

(*Flat*) What?

GIRL

(*Flat*) What? What is it?

MAN

Did you like our little performance? Our intermezzo a due? (*Before they can answer*) Ah! But where's baby-poo?

GIRL

(*Flat*) Asleep; all fed.

BOY

(*Licks lips*) I got dessert.

WOMAN

(*False hearty*) Oh, you have a baby!

BOY

Yes.

WOMAN

What kind?

BOY

(*Eyeing her*) A small one.

WOMAN

Aha. (*Exits left; false stealth*)

BOY

(*To* MAN) What do you want?

MAN

(*Cheerless smile*) What do we *want*. Well, I would imagine we want what almost everybody wants—eternal life, in great health, no older than we are when we want it; easy money, with enough self-deception to make us feel we've earned it, are worthy people; a government that lets us do whatever we want, serves our private interests and lets us feel we're doing all we can for . . . how do they call it—the less fortunate?; a bigger dick, a more muscular vagina; a baby, perhaps?

BOY

No, no. (*Articulated*) What do you *want?*

MAN

Hm?

BOY

Here; what do you want *here?*

MAN

(*Helpless gesture; false*) I'm not sure that I . . .

BOY

You're *here*.

MAN

(*Grudging*) Yes.

BOY

That . . . woman is here—is with you.

MAN

Everything being *rel*ative . . .

BOY

Yes.

GIRL

(*Suspicious*) Where *is* she? Where's she *gone!?* (WOMAN *re-enters, from stage right, very casually, an "O.K." finger gesture to* MAN, *a broad wink to him.*) Oh, *there* she is.

MAN

(*To* BOY) We are both here; yes.

BOY

(*Level*) Why?

MAN

Hm?

BOY

(*Still level, if harder*) Why are you here? What do you want?

MAN

(*Cheerless smile*) What do we *want*. Well, it's really very simple. We've come to take the baby.

(*Silence*)

BOY

What do you mean!?

MAN

(*Flat*) We've come to take the baby.

(*Shorter silence*)

GIRL

(*A look of panic*) What do you mean "you've come to take . . ."
Oh, my *God*! (*Suddenly exits, left*)

BOY

(*Eyes on* MAN; *steely*) I don't understand you.

WOMAN

He doesn't understand you; be clearer.

MAN

(*To* WOMAN) I thought I was being clear. (*To* BOY) What is it
you don't understand? The noun "baby"? The verb "take"?

WOMAN

You're not being nice.

MAN

You told me to be clear—clearer.

WOMAN

They're not mutually exclusive.

MAN

(*Heavy sigh*) *All* right. (*To* BOY) The baby. The baby?

BOY

(*Very innocent*) Yes?

MAN

(*Demonstrates*) We've come to take it.

BOY

I don't . . .

MAN

(*Very explicit*) A-way; a-way.

GIRL

(*Re-enters from left; hysterical*) WHERE'S THE BABY?!
WHAT HAVE YOU DONE WITH THE BABY?!

(*Silence*)

MAN

What baby?

(*Silence*)

WOMAN

Yes; what baby?

(*Tableau*)

END OF ACT ONE

Act Two

(No one on stage; otherwise everything as it was at the end of Act One)

MAN

(Enters, waves a little to audience. To someone) Is this where I was at the end of one—Act One? Right about here? *(Takes exact position as of the end of Act One. Generally; out)* Yes? Good. *(To stragglers)* Hurry back in, now; you don't want to miss the exposition. Well, maybe you do. *(Irritated complaint)* "Honestly! You'd think they'd have it in the *first* act!" *(Thinks about it)* No; you couldn't possibly. Well, let me tell you: intermissions are never long enough, are they. Did you enjoy yourselves while you were out for your cigarettes, or whatever? *(Wrinkles his nose, etc.)* Don't smoke; bad for you. Half a million die of it every year. In this country alone, subsidized murder. Not *you*, of course—someone you know. So; you had your cigarette, or your drink—not *quite* so bad, one or two a day good for the old heart, they say. *Or* your coffee. *(Harpy; shrill)* KEEP AWAKE! KEEP AWAKE! Or merely . . . stretching your legs, having a pee. *(Annoyed woman imitation)* "You'd think they'd build the ladies' restrooms bigger; after all these years you'd think they'd have noticed the lines! *Honestly!*" Or maybe just a phone call? Or a talk with friends—*or* strangers. Whatever. *(Shift of tone)* I must tell you something here: I have a troubling sense of what should be—rather than what *is*. It chokes me up at simpleminded movies—where good things

happen to good people? My throat clots, and I think I'm going
to cry. Because I know it can never happen in what they call
"real life"? Good things to good people and happy endings? That
it's all . . . fantasy? Is that what allows me to believe? To weep
in relief? If I saw it *really* happening—all good things to all good
people?—would I turn away in horror? Yes, probably: because it
could all . . . stop, could go away, be a single instant of glory, des-
perately cruel. We can't take glory because it shows us the abyss.
That is why we cry at movies—because it's *safe* to; it's all so . . .
beautifully false. But I have, as I say, this sense of what should
be rather than what is. And I file it away; file it away under "un-
wanted on the voyage, dangerous cargo," for I know it does not
apply? Because it is an impediment to . . . what do they say? . . .
to "getting through it all"? (*Smiles grimly; demonstrates shud-
dering*) It's troubling, though, I *tell* you. As . . . (*gestures*) . . . as
in, well . . . *here*; now; all this. Troubling, but I'll get through it.
(*Snaps fingers*) O.K.!! So, where did we leave off? "We've come
to take the baby." "I don't understand." "What baby?" etc. That
was it . . . casual—more or less—straightforward, but casual.
"We've come to take the baby." Remember it? Good. We'll see
if they let us take the baby from them. (*In*) Where were we all?
(*Off*) Will you come back in now? (BOY *and* GIRL *re-enter from
left,* WOMAN *from right; they take positions identical to their
positions on* MAN's "O.K. *Let's get on with it*") Fine. (*To* BOY *and*
GIRL) Now you two say "What?" "What is it?" You first, then her,
flat, flat, both of you. Say it! "What?" "What is it?" (*Pause*) Say
it, for God's sake!

BOY

(*Flat*) What?

GIRL

(*Flat*) What? What is it?

MAN

(*Approving*) That's right; that's it. (*False hearty*) Good to see
you! But where's "the little one"?

GIRL

(*Flat*) Asleep; all fed.

BOY

(*Licks lips*) I got dessert.

WOMAN

(*Quiet aside to* MAN) Oh, I get it. (*To* GIRL; *false hearty*) Oh, you have a baby!

GIRL

Yes.

WOMAN

What kind?

GIRL

(*Eyeing her*) A small one.

WOMAN

Aha. (*Quick aside to* MAN) Is this where I . . . (*answering her own question*) . . . yes; yes, it is. (*To* GIRL) A*ha*! (*Exits left; false stealth*)

BOY

(*To* MAN) What do you want?

MAN

(*Sotto voce aside to audience*) I love this speech. (*To* BOY; *cheerless smile*) What do we *want*. Well, I would imagine we want what almost everybody wants—eternal life, in great health, no older than we are when we want it; easy money, with enough self-deception to make us feel we've earned it, are worthy people; a government that lets us do whatever we want, serves our private interests and lets us feel we're doing all we can for . . . how do they call it—the less fortunate?; a bigger dick, a more muscular vagina; a baby, perhaps?

BOY

No, no. (*Articulated*) What do you *want*?

MAN

Hm?

BOY
Here; what do you want *here*?

MAN
(*Helpless gesture; false*) I'm not sure that I . . .

BOY
You're *here*.

MAN
(*Grudging*) Yes.

BOY
That . . . woman is here—is with you.

MAN
Everything being *rel*ative . . .

BOY
Yes.

GIRL
(*Suspicious*) Where *is* she? Where's she *gone!?* (WOMAN *re-enters, from stage right, very casually, an O.K. finger gesture to* MAN, *with a broad wink*) Oh, *there* she is.

MAN
(*To* BOY) We are both here; yes.

BOY
(*Level*) Why?

MAN
Hm?

BOY
(*Still level, if harder*) Why are you here? What do you want?

MAN
(*Cheerless smile*) What do we *want*. Well, it's really very simple. We've come to take the baby.
(*Silence*)

BOY

What do you mean?

MAN

(*Flat*) We've come to take the baby.
(*Shorter silence*)

GIRL

(*A look of panic*) What do you mean "you've come to take . . ."
Oh, my God!! (*Suddenly exits, left*)

BOY

(*Eyes on* MAN: *steely*) I don't understand you. (*Brief awareness
of* GIRL's *action*)

WOMAN

He doesn't understand you; be clearer.

MAN

(*To* WOMAN) I thought I was being clear. (*To* BOY) What is it
you don't understand? The noun "baby"? The verb "take"?

WOMAN

You're not being nice.

MAN

You told me to be clear—clearer.

WOMAN

They're not mutually exclusive.

MAN

(*Heavy sigh*) *All* right. (*To* BOY) The baby. The baby?

BOY

(*Very innocent*) Yes?

MAN

(*Demonstrates*) We've come to take it.

BOY

I don't . . .

MAN

(*Very explicit; impatient*) A-way; a-way.

GIRL

(*Re-enters from left; hysterical*) WHERE'S THE BABY??!!
WHAT HAVE YOU DONE WITH THE BABY??!!

(*Silence*)

MAN

What baby?

(*Silence*)

WOMAN

Yes; *what* baby?

MAN

(*Out, then in*) *There* we are! *Here* we go!

GIRL

WHAT HAVE YOU DONE WITH MY BABY??!!

BOY

(*Gathering energy; clearly about to lunge*) Look, you motherfucker, what have you done to . . .

MAN

(*A stopping hand up; very loud*) STOP!! (BOY *freezes*)

GIRL

(*Sobbing*) What have you done with my baby?

MAN

(*Loud*) BOTH OF YOU!! NOW JUST STOP!!

(GIRL *whimpers, sobs, but stays still;* BOY *puts his arm around her, never
taking his eyes off* MAN)

WOMAN

(*Distaste*) Such a performance! You'd think somebody was hurting somebody—or something!

MAN

(*Keeping his eyes on* BOY; *casual tone*) Wouldn't you?

WOMAN

You'd think something was amiss, as they say.

MAN

(*Ibid*) Wouldn't you?

GIRL

(*Weepy*) I want my baby.

MAN

Everyone wants his baby.

WOMAN

Her baby.

MAN

(*Shrugs*) Whatever. (*To* WOMAN; *points at* GIRL: *innocence*) *Her* baby? Everyone wants her baby?

WOMAN

(*Chuckles*) No, no; generics again.

BOY

(*About to get up, move toward* MAN) Okay. I've had enough of this now! What the fuck have you done with . . .

MAN

(*Hand up*) Hold!

BOY

(*Beginning to move*) I will not "hold," whatever that means.

WOMAN

(*Helpful*) It's Elizabethan.

BOY

(*Confused*) It's . . . it's *what*?!

MAN

ELIZABETHAN!! Now go sit down. If you care about this baby you behave yourself, yourselves. (*Demonstrates*) If there are two hands—see? two hands?—if there are two hands, we have the upper one. If you have ever had a baby—

BOY

If?

MAN

. . . if that is mother's milk you've been feeding on, and if you wish to see your real or imagined baby again—ever!—

BOY

Real? Or . . .

MAN

. . . if you are wiser than your years, be good.

(BOY *does so*)

WOMAN

(*To* MAN) You have a way with children.

MAN

As it was with my own.

WOMAN

Oh? You have children?

MAN

Certainly; I have six.

WOMAN

Really!

MAN

Yes: two black, two white, one green, and the other . . . well, I'm not certain, or I've lost track, or whatever.

BOY

(*Quietly*) Bullshit.

WOMAN

(*Ignoring* BOY) Two black?

MAN

Yes.

WOMAN

Half black, half white, what in the bad old days they used to call mulatto?

MAN

No; all black.

WOMAN

But . . .

MAN

This was when I was black.

WOMAN

Aha. Was this before you were white? Before . . .

MAN

No; it shifted: two white, one black, one green, et cetera.

WOMAN

I see; I see.

GIRL

(*To* MAN) You have no children.

MAN

Well, that may be, or may have been, or . . . whatever.

WOMAN

(*To* GIRL) Why do you say that?

GIRL

(*To* WOMAN) Nor do you.

WOMAN

Oh?

GIRL

No one who has children . . .

MAN

Had!

GIRL

(*Onward*) . . . would treat us like this—anyone like this.

BOY

She's right, you know. (*Pause*) Had?

MAN

(*Playful*) Well, *having* had doesn't mean one *has*. (*Pause*) Does it?

WOMAN

One green?

MAN

Yes. (*Out*) Does this need explaining?

WOMAN

When you were green?

MAN

(*Back in; thinks a moment*) Well, when *some*one was.

WOMAN

Half green then.

GIRL

(*Soft, gentle pleading*) Please? (BOY *quietly shushes her*)

MAN

(*Considers it*) Mmmmm . . . light green. (*To* BOY *and* GIRL)
So, I want you to understand I know about children, about
who has them . . . and who does *not*; how large they may be,
how many legs they have—if they have the number they are
supposed to, where they come out of—the length of the small
intestine in a two-week-old . . .

WOMAN

How long?

MAN

Eleven and three-quarter inches. The color of loss, the names
most commonly not used . . . all the things essential. You don't
fool with *me*. Fool yourselves, fool each *other*, but don't try it
with *me*. *I've* touched the golden dick. Have *you*? (*To* BOY,
specifically) *Have* you? *Have* you? You there?

BOY

(*Preoccupied*) Have I what?

MAN

Touched the golden dick.

BOY

I don't know what you're talking about, mister. (*Suddenly
loud*) Where's our baby!!??

MAN/WOMAN

(*Softly singing*) Yes, Sir, where's our baby? No, Sir, we don't
mean maybe. Yes, Sir, where's our baby now?

MAN

(*Speaking again*) Too bad about the dick—the golden dick.
(*As* BOY *prepares to lunge*) I'd be careful if I were you!
(BOY *lunges; Man flips him on his back on the floor with a judo move;
pins* BOY's *neck under his foot*)

MAN

I said I'd be careful if I were you! (*To* GIRL) Are you going to
try something, too? (GIRL *sobs, shakes her head*) Good; the
lady here is adept at things as well.

WOMAN

I am.

MAN

Everyone's adept at something. (*To pinned* BOY) Will you be good?

BOY

Yes.

MAN

Good. (BOY *gets up, not easily*) Go to your chair. (BOY *does;* GIRL *moves to comfort him*) Good. Touching. (*To* WOMAN) Goodness, I'm saying "good" a lot, *aren't* I?

WOMAN

(*Shrugs*) It *sounds* right.

MAN

Good! (*To* BOY *and* GIRL) So! No more shenanigans. (*Out*) Is that Irish? Shenanigans? (*If anyone answers, handle it; in any event, go on with this*) I looked it up once in the dictionary and it didn't say; it said "informal," which I don't believe is a genesis. Though maybe it is . . . the island of informality? The city of shenanigan? I meant to look it up somewhere else, but I . . . lost interest, I guess. (*Back in*) In any event, (*To* BOY *and* GIRL) no more (*very pronounced*) she-nan-i-gans. No?

BOY

(*Nursing his neck*) No.

MAN

No what?

BOY

No more.

MAN

No more *what*!?

BOY

No more shenanigans.

MAN

Always be precise: saves time, saves paper. Did I hurt you?

BOY

No.

MAN

No wound?

BOY

No.

MAN

(*To* BOY *and* GIRL) If you have no wounds, how can you know
if you're alive? If you have no scar, how do you know who you
are? Have been?

BOY

(*Impatient*) Come on, mister!

WOMAN

(*To* BOY) Listen to him.

MAN

(*To* BOY) Was your fracture compound? Did it stick out
through the skin—like snapped wood?

GIRL

(*To* BOY; *shy*) *Did* it?

BOY

No!

MAN

If it didn't, who *are* you? Who have you ever *been*? (*To* GIRL)
Was it a caesarean for the baby? A theoretical caesarean for
the theoretical baby?

BOY

Theor . . .

GIRL

No! No wound!

MAN

(*To them both*) Blood? Piercings? Gougings? Wounds, children; wounds. Without wounds what *are* you? You're too young for the batterings time brings us . . .

WOMAN

(*Dramatic*) Oh, God! The batterings!

MAN

(*To* WOMAN) . . . time brings us.

WOMAN

Sorry! . . . time brings us. (*An aside*) Oh, God?

MAN

One is enough. (*To* BOY) Give me your arm; let me see your wound.

BOY

(*Self-protective*) Hah! You think I'll fall for that!?

MAN

Oh, I wouldn't break your arm; *I* don't want you on your knees—not literally. Ever? No, I don't think so. Break your arm? Nahhhh! Your heart, perhaps. Your heart, yes. Certainly your heart.

WOMAN

(*Pleased*) Oh, the heart!

MAN

Give me your heart, then; I'll break *that*. If you don't have the wound of a broken heart, how can you know you're alive? If you have no broken heart, how do you know who you are? Have been? Can ever be?

GIRL

(*To* MAN *and* WOMAN; *crying a little*) Leave us alone? Please, let me have my baby?

MAN

(*Sighs*) We're going to have to talk about this. (*Beginning of lecture*) What is a baby? (*Out*) What is a baby? (*In and out, now*) We must, first of all, define a baby. A baby . . . *what*!? A baby mouse? A baby kangaroo? A baby wolverine? A baby . . . *baby*. A human baby, an almost, not quite yet human baby— no larger than, well, somewhat larger than that "great divide." (*To* BOY) Hey? Between the something slopes, or something?

BOY

(*Curt*) What?

MAN

Nothing. (*In and out again*) You can't go home again? Surely not! They say we want to go back in—back home—some of us, at any rate. Try it! A minute after out-you-slide—or whatever—it's all closing up, closing down, till the next time. Push you back in—head first, whatever? Wouldn't work! The water's gone now; you've been shocked into breathing . . . what? Nothing *you* can see, *could* see if you had *eyes*—eyes that *opened*. (*Bravura quote*) "Oh, blessed eyes that never ope!" (*Natural again*) "Ope"; I've always liked "ope."

WOMAN

(*Matter-of-fact*) You're running on.

MAN

Yes? I am?

WOMAN

"What is a baby?" Then relate *that* to where we are—to this.

MAN

Aha!

GIRL

(*Quiet*) Please? My baby?

MAN

(*Hearty*) Now, look; if there *is* a baby, and if it is yours, and you can prove it's yours, we'll handle it.

BOY

(*Ominously quiet*) If? Who *are* you? Who are you, really?

GIRL

Yes; who *are* you?

MAN

(*To* BOY) I am your destination. Remember? Is that familiar? (*To* WOMAN) Now you.

WOMAN

(*Tiny orienting pause; to* GIRL) Yes. Yes, I go in the back with you, and I am your destination.

MAN

(*To* BOY) We do things together, you and I, that no one else has done.

WOMAN

(*To* GIRL) You love me; we are each other's . . . whatever.

GIRL

(*Intense; to* BOY) None of this is true!

MAN

(*To* BOY) The first time you touched me . . . (*Indicates*) there, I almost fainted. It was so . . . unexpected, I suppose.

BOY

(*Cold*) You fuck!

MAN

(*Considers*) Well . . . yes.

WOMAN

(*To* GIRL; *dreamy*) We lay there, you and I, true spoons, the two of us, mouths on each other . . .

GIRL

(*Voice shaking*) No! No!

MAN

(*To* BOY) We are each other's destination. No? Yes?

WOMAN

(*To* GIRL) No? We are not?

MAN

(*To both* BOY *and* GIRL) Or are we Gypsies? Hm?

GIRL

(*To* BOY; hysterical) They're Gypsies!!

BOY

(*Eyes on* MAN; *steely, to comfort*) No; no, they're not.

MAN

(*Pretending bewilderment*) We're *not*!?

BOY

No!

MAN

(*Of* WOMAN) You don't recognize her fedora and her huge mustache?

WOMAN

(*To* GIRL) You came to me; you brought your life savings in a paper bag.

GIRL

No! I don't *have* any life savings!

BOY

(*Pleading; explaining*) We're very young.

MAN

And therefore you don't have Gypsies? (*To* GIRL) *She* had a Gypsy.

WOMAN

(*To* GIRL) Yes, you *went* to one. (*Uncertain*) Was it *me*? Was it to me?

BOY

But it wasn't for *that*.

MAN

For *what*?

GIRL

For . . . life savings, and all.

MAN

Well, I should hope not. How dumb can you be?!

WOMAN

(*To* MAN, *about* GIRL) That's for *later*, when you *get* dumb, life-savings-time dumb.

MAN

(*Sighs*) Time; time, the great leveler. (*To* BOY; *sweet*) Tell me *about* you; tell us your history. (*Whispered aside; out*) Exposition.

BOY

(*Confused*) Who? Me?

MAN

(*Back in*) Whatever. You can tell us your history, or she can tell us your history, and you can tell us hers, and we won't know *what* to disbelieve.

BOY

(*A recitation; quiet rage*) I'm a twenty-three-year-old white, Anglo-Saxon American man . . .

MAN

That's a redundancy. All Anglo-Saxons are white.

BOY

Yes? A twenty-three-year-old Anglo-Saxon American man.

MAN

Boy.

BOY

Boy—yes?—boy, and I'm married to *her*, the light of my life.

WOMAN

Your destination.

BOY

(*Confused*) What?

WOMAN

(*Cheerful*) Your destination! Don't you remember?

MAN

(*To* BOY) I thought it was you and me: that time you touched
me . . . (*Gestures*) here, and put your lips to my . . .

BOY

(*Loud enough to cover*) THE LIGHT OF MY LIFE!

MAN/WOMAN

(*As if on cue*) Roll me over, in the clover,
                Roll me over, lay me down, and do it again.

MAN

(*To* BOY *and* GIRL) Familiar? No?

BOY

(*Shaking his head*) What more do you want? When will you . . .

MAN

(*Expansive*) Ohhhhh, *much* more.

GIRL

(*Sudden*) I want my baby!

WOMAN

(*Groucho*) Everybody wants his baby—her baby—whatever.

MAN

(*To* BOY) Tell us more; tell us what we want to know, and then tell us what we *don't*. *I'd* like to know, for example, why you took up with this young woman, when you obviously despise her.

BOY

(*Rage; frustration*) I *love* her; I love her with all my *heart*!

WOMAN

(*To* MAN; *false support of* BOY) He *loves* her; she loves *him*.

MAN

(*To* WOMAN) Well, *that* may be—that she loves *him*. (*To* BOY) *You* love *her*?

BOY

YES!!

MAN

Tisk, tisk, tisk! Then, what shall I think of the letter you sent me when we were apart . . .

BOY

We were never together!

MAN

. . . when we were apart, saying it was all for show, that her family has money, you can't stand the smell of her, the things she makes you do, and . . .

BOY

(*Making to lunge*) You motherfucking . . . !!

MAN

(*Warning hand up instantly*) Hanh!! The baby? Remember the baby?

BOY

(*Subsiding*) You . . .

MAN

Yes: *me*. I am the one, am I not? Am I not the gypsy you love, on your knees before me? Do you not aspire to my huge mustache, to my fedora?

BOY

(*Heavy sigh*) I don't know you, mister.

MAN

(*Out*) They all say that.

WOMAN

(*Attorney; to* GIRL) Did you not fake pregnancy to . . . to get him for yourself?

GIRL

No! No! I didn't! We married and *then* I got pregnant!

WOMAN

(*Out*) They all say that.

BOY

(*Quietly*) She was a virgin.

MAN

(*Tiny pause; to* BOY) When?

BOY

When I married her; when I met her.

MAN

Which came first?

BOY

(*Bewildered*) What?!

WOMAN

(*Helping*) He means: Did you marry her and *then* meet her, or . . .

BOY

NO!

MAN

No, you did not marry her before you met her, or you did not meet her before you married her?

BOY

(*Hands to ears*) *Stop* it!

GIRL

(*To* BOY; *very shy*) *Did* you write him a letter?

BOY

(*Exploding*) I don't *know* the man!!

MAN

(*To* GIRL; soothing) A fan letter; fans often write to those they've never met. Hope; hope!

WOMAN

(*Echo*) Hope.

GIRL

(*To* BOY; *determined*) *Did* you?!

BOY

(*To* GIRL; *pleading*) Of *course* not! I *love* you.

MAN

(*To* BOY; *explaining*) I was one of the Gypsy boys who stopped you on your way back from the gym-gym.

WOMAN

(*Nods happily*) And I was another.

MAN

I was the one who stopped in front of you, the one who spoke to you . . .

WOMAN

(*As if quoting*) You're the one who put the guard dogs on us, *aren't* you.

BOY

(*Memory; rote*) Guards, not guard dogs.

GIRL

(*Shakes her head; memory*) Not a wise answer.

WOMAN

You guys could have paid, you said.

GIRL

Nor that.

BOY

(*Dreamy*) I did?

MAN

Yes, you did, and no hard feelings, you said.

BOY

(*Ibid*) I did?

WOMAN

Yes; yes, you did.

BOY

(*Recalling, still dreamy*) And I put my arm out . . .

WOMAN

. . . and you put your arm out . . .

MAN

. . . and you put your arm out . . . and CRACK!!!

WOMAN

Crack!

GIRL

Crack!

BOY

It hurt so; it hurt so very much.

(GIRL *takes his shoulder to comfort him; he swivels to his knees beside her chair.*)

MAN

And I came up to you . . .

WOMAN

. . . and I came up to you, and I undid my fly and (*A trifle uncertain*) what was I going to do?

BOY

I don't know. You're going to piss on me?

MAN

Or maybe it was me, and you know what *I* wanted, what *you* wanted.

WOMAN

(*Echo*) What *you* wanted.

BOY

Or maybe . . . or maybe . . .

GIRL

(*Offers her breast to* BOY) Here; here.

BOY

Maybe he *wasn't* going to piss on me. Maybe he was going to . . .

GIRL

Here!! (BOY *takes her breast in his mouth; brief tableau*)

WOMAN

(*Unemphasized fact*) That is so . . . touching.

MAN

Yes; yes, it is.

MAN/WOMAN
Roll me over, in the clover,
Roll me over, lay me down, and do it again.

WOMAN

That is so . . . touching.

MAN

Yes; yes, it is. (*Brief pause; slaps hands together*) O.K.! Back
to work!

(*Boy disattaches himself; Girl replaces breast*)

WOMAN
(*To* BOY) Why did you never do that to me? I know you wanted to.

BOY

Pardon? (*Wiping lips*)

WOMAN
I was eighteen, wasn't I, and moving into ripeness? And I had
been to Europe and I knew the women there went without
bras if their breasts were exemplary and if they were young,
and I had my lovely breasts? (*Cups them for him*) Lovely?
Breasts? (*Tiny pause*) Nothing?

BOY
(*A quick look to see how* GIRL *is reacting*) Lady, I . . .

WOMAN
Didn't you want to suck them? Everyone else did . . . wanted to.

MAN

Of course he did.

WOMAN
(*To* BOY) Of course you did; of course you wanted to. You said
you would paint me; you said you were a painter.

BOY

Lady . . .

WOMAN

You said you would paint me . . . naked, my lovely breasts, the
dimple of my belly, my milk-pink hips, my burning bush?
(GIRL *begins to weep*)

MAN

(*Scoffing*) Milk-pink?

WOMAN

(*A trifle defensive*) Well . . . yes. (*To* BOY) You were only one
of my lovers, of course, one of the sturdy, virile boys, the
young and handsome, well-muscled . . .

GIRL

(*To* BOY; *rage and tears*) You know her!!

BOY

(*Trying to comfort her; dogmatic*) No! No, I don't know her!

MAN

(*To no one*) Oh what a wangled teb we weave.

WOMAN

A what?

MAN

A teb; a wangled teb.

WOMAN

What is *that*?

MAN

You remember. He was only one of your lovers, no?

WOMAN

Hm? Oh! Oh; right. (*To* BOY) You were a *splendid* lover,
though . . . slow, patient, thoughtful, but always in command,
and driving . . .

GIRL

(*To* BOY; *still weeping*) You *know* her!

BOY

(*Pounding his fists on his knees*) I do *not*! I do *not* know her!

MAN

(*To* WOMAN, *but so* GIRL *will hear*) When *was* all this? When were you two lovers?

WOMAN

(*With a toss of her hand*) Oh . . . last year, last month, last week, on his way to seeing her at the hospital, on his way from seeing her at the hospital—her and the baby. Earlier today.

MAN

The so-called baby.

WOMAN

(*Smiles*) The so-called baby.

BOY

(*Quiet intensity; almost crying*) I don't know you! I've never been with anyone but her.

MAN

(*To* WOMAN) Tell me about his penis; compare notes, so to speak. Show her you know the man through his manhood.

BOY

(*Flustered rage*) She's never seen my penis!

WOMAN

(*About to begin*) Well, all right now, let me see: I've seen penie in my life, and on a scale of one to ten—ten being *very* un-*likely*—I would say that he was a . . . oh, a . . .

GIRL

(*Exuberant in her invention*) He doesn't have one! She couldn't have seen it because he doesn't have one! So there!!

BOY

(GIRL *nudges him*) Right! She's right! So there!

GIRL

So there!! (*Giggles*)

MAN

(*Out*) They are so inventive, these two. (*Back in; to* BOY *and* GIRL) In the sense that the Queen of Spain does not have legs?

BOY

(*Cold*) What?

MAN

(*Out; pleasant*) It is said that once, centuries ago, an envoy from the East came to the Spanish court—with gifts, of course, gifts for the royal family, including fine-spun silk, a novelty back then. "For her Majesty," the envoy said, in his—well, his silkiest tone. (WOMAN *chuckles appreciatively*) Thank you. "For her Majesty, silk for her Majesty's legs." The major domo—or whatever he was—their Majesty's major-domo, sniffed, the story goes, raised his eyebrows at the effrontery, the familiarity, and said, in his haughtiest tone, "The Queen of Spain does not have . . . legs." (*Back in; to* BOY *and* GIRL) Is that the sense you mean, that your young man does not have a penis in the sense that the Queen of Spain does not have legs? Or are we dealing here with a bewildering and somber deformity, one which puts into even greater question the matter of a baby?

WOMAN

(*Rather puzzled*) That's something you'd think I would have noticed—or not noticed, rather.

BOY

(*Pause*) Go fuck yourselves.

MAN

Right on! (*He and* WOMAN *slap each other's right palms.* GIRL *tries to sneak off, with an "it's O.K." gesture to* BOY. MAN *notices; a warning*) I wouldn't do that!!! (GIRL *hesitates*) Leave the so-called baby be! *If* you have a baby—

BOY

I told you, we have a baby.

GIRL

Yes, we have a baby.

MAN

. . . if there *is* a baby, who is to say it has ever been yours?
Who is to say you have a right to it? Or that you didn't steal
it? Gypsies *do* steal things.

WOMAN

Yes; yes, they do.

MAN

(*To* GIRL; *very harsh*) So . . . SIDDDOWN!!

GIRL

(*Sitting; weeping quietly*) We are not Gypsies.

BOY

("*Will this help?*") No; no, we're not.

WOMAN

Well . . . *some*one is.

MAN

(*Seemingly puzzled*) Yes; yes, that's right . . . *some*one is, *must*
be. (*To* GIRL; *steely*) If you can prove it is yours—belongs to you
. . . you did not steal it, as Gypsies do . . . belongs to *you* . . .

WOMAN

(*Helping*) . . . and belongs *with* you . . .

MAN

(*To* WOMAN) Yes; right; thank you.

WOMAN

Welcome.

GIRL

I *told* you . . .

BOY

She *told* you . . .

MAN

(*To* GIRL *again*) . . . belongs to you, *and* belongs *with* you, then your interest in seeing it *ever* transcends your need to see it now. (*Pause*) No?

GIRL

(*Still quietly weeping*) Yes; yes, it does.

MAN

Good girl; you'll go far—to paraphrase.

BOY

I'll ask you one more time, mister, and only once more, who do you . . .

MAN

(*To* BOY *and* GIRL) No; the question is not who I think I am, but who I cannot be—the knowledge we all have of who we all cannot be, singularly, of course. I've lived long enough to understand that *that* is the most important question. Keep it in mind as you go on through it—both of you: what we cannot do; who we cannot be.

(WOMAN *begins signing—clearly absurd signing-like gestures*)

MAN

What are you doing?

WOMAN

Signing.

MAN

You know *how*? You know how to *sign*?

WOMAN

(*Signing*) It would seem so.

MAN
When did you learn? And *why*? *Why* did you learn?

WOMAN
(*Shrugs; signs*) It came upon me.

MAN
When?

WOMAN
Just now; I just realized I could do it.

MAN
Sign away.

WOMAN
(*Signing; smiling*) Thank you.

MAN
(*Out now*) Ignore her; I mean pay attention if you want to, but concentrate on *me*. I am talking; she is listening. Well, she is talking, too, in a way, but following *me*. She listens and then talks, almost simultaneously, but not quite. I . . . *talk*. I even listen as I *talk*—to myself, not to her. I can't sign. (WOMAN *stops signing*) You've stopped.

WOMAN
It comes and goes. I've suddenly forgotten. You go on; I'll catch up.

MAN
(*Scoffs*) With *me*? Never! (*Out again*) So. Who I cannot be. (*To* BOY *and* GIRL) Learn from this, children. (*Out again*) I cannot be young again; I cannot be a woman—therefore I cannot have babies, blah, blah, blah, if indeed I *would* have them, or *could*. (*To* GIRL) Eh, toots?

GIRL
Leave me alone!

BOY

(*Gentle pleading*) Leave her alone.

MAN

(*To* GIRL) But you *asked* . . . or *he* did: who I thought I was, et cetera. (*In and out now*) I would like, above all else, to be . . . historical and free-floating; I regret the people I have not met. I regret Jesus most of all. God! The questions! That's in retrospect, of course . . . mostly. Still: to *really* . . . *hear* him. (*To* BOY *and* GIRL, *who just look back*) How many sentences do the scholars think are his in the testaments? Three? A half-dozen? (*Dismissive gesture; back out*) No education. To have *been* there; to have heard him speak. (*To* WOMAN) This is important.

WOMAN

I know, I know; I'll try. (*Begins signing again, badly, then better*).

MAN

(*In and out again; ecstatic*) The Sermon on the Mount! Oh, my God! One could dine out on that . . . *forever*! The truth about the Last Supper? I almost don't dare mention the Crucifixion! Would I have tried to stop it? Would He have made me *not*? Not tried? Was it what he wanted? The proof he needed?

WOMAN

(*Stops signing*) You go too far!

MAN

(*Apologetic*) I know, I know; madness lies that way.

GIRL

(*Quiet begging*) Please?

MAN

(*To* GIRL) Soon; soon, now. (*To himself, mostly; shakes head*) All the things I know I can never be, can never do, can never . . . *undo*. That's the worst. (*Ponders*) All the things I can never be (*Harsher now, to* BOY *and* GIRL), including as sympathetic as you would like to your . . . what?—your "plight"? Your supposed *plight*? You who are probably not what you say you are—*who* you say you are.

BOY

(*Weary*) I've told you . . . a hundred times . . .

MAN

Yes yes yes, I know; you're married—to one another . . . you
have this baby.

BOY

Yes!

GIRL

Yes!

MAN

(*Dismissive*) Right; sure; and the Gypsies have taken it—or
will, or have thought about it, at the very least, as Gypsies will.

(GIRL *weeps;* BOY *takes her hand*)

BOY

(*Very serious; very calm*) The baby is real; the baby is ours; we
went to the hospital for her to have it. (GIRL *nods, still weeping a little*)

WOMAN

You go to the hospital a *lot.*

MAN

(*Remembering*) Yes! Yes, you do! You came to *see* me; I was
on the stretcher; I was unconscious . . .

WOMAN

(*To* MAN; *of* BOY) . . . and he said to himself: "When he wakes
up—*if* he wakes up—I'm going to be there . . . "

MAN

. . . and I'll be the first person he sees, and he'll love me; he'll
want me and he'll love me; he's my destination.

WOMAN

And he told them he was your brother.

MAN

(*To* BOY) And I woke up, and you were hard.

GIRL

It was me!

BOY

It was her!

GIRL

It was me!

MAN

(*Pause*) Oh?

WOMAN

(*Pause*) Oh?

BOY

(*Dogged; almost in tears*) Yes; yes. It was her; she woke up and I was hard.

MAN

(*Surprise*) It wasn't me?! *I* remember you being hard.

WOMAN

(*To* BOY) We all do; we all remember you being hard.

MAN

Dick or no.

WOMAN

Dick or no.

MAN

And out popped the baby, the so-called baby?

BOY

When?

MAN

Then!

WOMAN

When-then.

BOY

No; that was when we *met*!

MAN

I remember; I woke up; the nurse said you were my brother,
and you were hard.

BOY

(*More dogged*) No! Not then then; not that time! When we
went to have the baby!

MAN

(*Distant*) I don't remember. Was it me? I don't remember.

WOMAN

Maybe it was *me*.

BOY

(*To prove his existence;* GIRL *cries softly during this*) I was in
the kitchen, and she came in and she said, "My water broke;
my water just broke!"

WOMAN

It *was* me! Yes; of course.

BOY

And I bundled her up, and we took a cab to the hospital. I
called our baby doctor, and we raced off to the hospital.

MAN

(*Shakes his head*) Everyone's a baby—even the doctor.

WOMAN

(*To* BOY) It isn't *water*, you know. (*To* GIRL) It isn't water.

BOY

(*Determined*) . . . and it wasn't long; it didn't take very long.

MAN

(*Remembering giving birth*) But it hurt! Oh, my God, it hurt!
How it hurt me!

WOMAN

(*Remembering*) Oh, God, how it hurt me!

BOY

(*Ibid*) And I held her hand during it, and *I* squeezed and *she*
squeezed . . .

(GIRL *begins howling birthing sounds now, punctuating* BOY's *speech; she
stays seated; shows no emotion, hands in lap—merely howling*)

BOY

. . . and she howled . . . and she howled . . . and she howled . . .
and the sound was terrible, but I held on, *we* held on . . . the
doctor and the nurses were all there . . . and the blood . . . and
the blood came, and I'd never seen so much . . . blood, and
then the baby came, the baby's head came (GIRL *ceases howling*) . . . and the rest of it . . .

GIRL

(*Hands going wide*) WOOOOOOSSSSSSH!!

MAN

(*Ecstasy*) . . . and I'd never seen so much blood!

WOMAN

(*Ecstasy*) . . . I felt it! The blood, and then the baby . . .

BOY

(*Ignoring them; maybe with a dismissive hand gesture*) . . .
and there it was; there was our baby.

GIRL

(*Softer*) Wooooosssssh.

WOMAN

(*Shakes her head*) Just like in the movies.

MAN

(*Agreeing; suddenly understanding*) Yes! (*To* BOY) You go to a
lot of movies?

BOY

(*Bewildered*) Who? This wasn't a movie!

WOMAN

It looked like one to *me*—all the trappings.

MAN

(*To* WOMAN) Yes! *Didn't* it? When I had *my* baby . . .

WOMAN

The black one?

MAN

No; the green one; there was very little blood, no pain . . .

WOMAN

Well, you had a spinal.

MAN

Hmmmm! Yes, that may have had something to do with it. In
any event, when I had *my* baby *I* had the Gypsies, too. The
Gypsies came to me, too.

WOMAN

(*Smiles*) Too?

MAN

(*Smiles*) Whatever. But I was wise. (*To* GIRL) When I took *my*
baby to the Gypsy . . .

WOMAN

The old Gypsy *woman*.

MAN

(*Aside, to* WOMAN) Whatever. (*To* GIRL *again*) When I took *my* baby to the Gypsy, *I* was smart; when they told me to put the baby in a big paper bag, *I* didn't *do* it.

GIRL

(*Weeping*) No! I *did*n't!

WOMAN

(*To* MAN) Of *course* you didn't!

MAN

(*Still to* GIRL) *I* didn't put it on the table, between me and the Gypsy.

WOMAN

Of course you didn't!

MAN

(*Still to* GIRL) *I* didn't see the lights go all funny, and hear the music.

WOMAN

Of course not!

MAN

(*Still to* GIRL) And *I* didn't take the bag and bury it in the back yard for three weeks, so the baby could double, or whatever.

WOMAN

(*Out*) Twins!

GIRL

No! I didn't!

BOY

She didn't!

WOMAN

(*To* MAN) Of course you didn't!

MAN

So that when it came time to dig it up . . .

GIRL

(*Weeping*) I . . . didn't . . . do . . . that!

BOY

(*Comforting her*) No; no; of course you didn't.

WOMAN

(*Observing*) Touching.

MAN

Or whatever.

GIRL

Please. My baby.

MAN

(*Pause; brisk now*) Well, time for the old blanket trick.

WOMAN

Oh; right! (*Exiting right; to* BOY *and* GIRL) I'll be right back.
(*Out*) I'll be right back.

MAN

(*To* BOY *and* GIRL, *as* GIRL *looks apprehensively off right*) She'll
be right back. (*Out*) She'll be right back.

BOY

(*After a pause; shy; quietly fearful*) Are you Gypsies?

MAN

(*Laughs; to* BOY) Do we look like Gypsies? Do we have fedoras and bushy mustaches . . . ?

BOY

Whatever, then. Have you come to hurt us? Beyond salvation?
Hurt us to the point that . . . if you want to do this to us, hurt
us so, ask *why*! Ask what we've *done*. I can take pain and loss

and all the rest *later*; I *think* I can—*we* can—when it comes
as natural as . . . sleep? But . . . now? Not now. We're happy;
we love each other; I'm hard all the time; we have a baby; we
don't even understand each other yet. So . . . give us some
time. (*Pause*) Please?

MAN

(*After long pause; brisk*) Time's up.

(WOMAN *re-enters with the baby blanket bundle, nuzzling.* GIRL *instinctively reaches toward bundle*)

WOMAN

(*Possessive*) AH!

(GIRL *withdraws*)

BOY

(*An echo from before*) Please?

MAN

(*Gentler*) Time's up. (WOMAN *hands him the bundle. Out; a barker*) Ladies and Gentlemen! See what we have here! The baby bundle! The old bundle of baby! (*Throws it up in the air, catches it;* GIRL *screams*)

BOY

(*Desperate*) Don't do *that*!

WOMAN

(*To* BOY; *comforting*) He knows what he's doing.

MAN

(*To* BOY *and* GIRL) I know what I'm doing. (*Out again; in when necessary*) The old baby bundle—treasure of treasures, light of our lives, purpose—they say—of all the fucking, all the . . . well, all the everything. Now the really good part, the part we've all been waiting for! (*He takes the bundle, snaps it open, displays both sides; we see there is nothing there.*) Shazaam! You see? Nothing! No baby! Nothing! (GIRL *goes to blanket;* MAN *gives it to her; she searches it, cuddles it; weeps. To* GIRL) You see? Nothing.

BOY

(*Pause*) You *have* decided then: you have decided to hurt us beyond salvation.

MAN

(*Objective*) I said: time's up.

BOY

No matter how young we are? No matter how . . .

WOMAN

(*Gentle*) He said: time's up.

MAN

I said: time's up. Wounds, children, wounds. If you have no wounds, how can you know you're alive? How can you know who you are? (BOY *bows his head. To* BOY *and* GIRL) Let us deal finally, once and for all, with the baby—I put it in quotes, "baby." I want you to be certain, you have a baby? Have ever *had* a baby. (*Pause*) You have a baby?

(GIRL *replies more and more tentatively;* BOY *stays firm*)

(*Don't rush this section*)

BOY

Yes.

GIRL

Yes.

(*Pause*)

MAN

You have a baby?

BOY

Yes.

GIRL

Yes.

(*Pause*)

WOMAN

You have a baby?

BOY

Yes.

GIRL

Yes.

(*Pause*)

MAN

You have a baby?

BOY

Yes.

GIRL

(*Opens mouth; closes it*)

BOY

(*Tiny pause*) Say something! (*She shakes her head*)
(*Increasing intensity, and increased tempo here*)

MAN

I'll ask you once again. You have a baby?

BOY

(*To* GIRL) Tell him.

GIRL

(*Finally*) I don't know.

BOY

Of course you know!

GIRL

No! I don't know!

MAN

Once more: you have a baby?

BOY

(*To* GIRL) *Tell* him!!

WOMAN

(*Gentle*) Tell me, too.

BOY

Tell her!

MAN

Tell *someone:* you have a baby?

GIRL

(*Long pause; finally; rather shy*) No; I don't think so.

BOY

But . . . ?

GIRL

(*To* BOY; *begging*) No; no; we don't have one; we don't have a baby.
(*Varying intensities and tempi*) Please, please, no baby, I can't . . .

BOY

(*Rage*) I was with you when it was born!

GIRL

(*Flat*) No.

BOY

No one before *me*; we *made* it!

MAN

(*An aside; quiet; out*) They all say that.

GIRL

(*Flat*) No.

BOY

I SAW IT! I HELD IT! I WATCHED IT COME OUT OF
YOU, ALL BLOOD . . . !

GIRL

No. Please; no.

WOMAN

(*To* GIRL) You have no baby.

GIRL

(*Flat*) No.

MAN

(*To* WOMAN) What a wise girl.

WOMAN

What a brave girl.

BOY

(*Crying now*) I . . . saw . . . it; I . . . I held it.
(*Response tempi easy now; all gentle except* BOY)

WOMAN

No.

MAN

No.

GIRL

No.

BOY

(*Sobbing*) Yes.

WOMAN

No.

MAN

No.

GIRL

No.

BOY

Yes.

WOMAN

No.

MAN

No.

GIRL

No.

BOY

No?

WOMAN

No.

MAN

No.

GIRL

No.

BOY

(*Pause*) No.

MAN

(*Sighs*) Well then; we're done.

WOMAN

Yes.

(MAN *and* WOMAN *begin moving upstage;* MAN *pauses; mild puzzled look;* BOY *and* GIRL *in silent tears—if possible*)

MAN

Tears! (*Out*) Tears! (*To* WOMAN) Tears!

WOMAN

(*Gentle smile*) Yes: tears.

MAN

(*To* BOY *and* GIRL, *who are too interior to respond*) Oh what a wangled teb we weave. Wounds, children, wounds. Learn from it. Without wounds, what are you? If you don't have a broken heart . . . (*Shrugs*) We'll leave you, then. Don't get up. (*Taking* WOMAN's *hand*) Shall we?

WOMAN

Shall we?
(*They exit; silence;* BOY *and* GIRL *still*)

BOY

(*Still in tears*) No baby?

GIRL

(*Still in tears*) No.

BOY

(*More a wish than anything*) I hear it crying!

GIRL

(*Please*) No; no, you don't.

BOY

(*Defeat*) No baby.

GIRL

(*Begging*) No. Maybe later? When we're older . . . when we can take . . . terrible things happening? Not now.

BOY

(*Pause*) I hear it crying.

GIRL

(*Pause; same tone as* BOY) I hear it too. I hear it crying too.
(*Lights fade*)

CURTAIN